All About Animals in the Snow

All About Polar Bears

Kerrily Sapet

EZ READERS
AN IMPRINT OF
MITCHELL LANE PUBLISHERS

CREATING YOUNG NONFICTION READERS

EZ Readers offer nonfiction for beginning readers in PreK through first grade, using simple language, clear illustrations, and engaging facts to build vocabulary and confidence.

TIPS FOR READING NONFICTION WITH BEGINNING READERS

Talk about Nonfiction

Begin by explaining that nonfiction books give us information that is true. The book will be organized around a specific topic or idea, and we may learn new facts through reading.

Look at the Parts

Most nonfiction books have helpful features. Our *EZ Readers* include color photographs and graphic aids, a table of contents, a glossary, and an index. Share the purpose of these features with your reader.

Color Photos and Graphic Aids

A lot of information can be found by "reading" photos, charts, maps, and other graphic aids found within nonfiction texts. Help your reader learn more about the different ways information can be displayed.

Table of Contents

Located at the front of the book, this list shows the big ideas within the text and the page numbers where they can be found.

Glossary

Located at the back of the book, the glossary defines key words and phrases that are related to the topic. These words and phrases can be found in the text in colored type.

Index

Located at the back of the book, an index is an alphabetical list of topics and the page numbers where they can be found.

With a little help and guidance about reading nonfiction, you can feel good about introducing a young reader to the world of *EZ Readers* nonfiction books.

EZ Readers is an imprint of:

Mitchell Lane
PUBLISHERS

2001 SW 31st Avenue
Hallandale, FL 33009
mitchelllanepub.com

First Edition, 2026.

Author: Kerrily Sapet
Editor: Morgan Brody

ISBN 979-8-89260-851-0 (library binding)
ISBN 979-8-90145-044-4 (paperback)
ISBN 979-8-89260-948-7 (ebook)

LC record available at https://lccn.loc.gov/2025950879

Photo credits: Adobe, Pixasquare, cover, 1, 2, 3, 4, 8, 12, 15,19, 21, 22, 23, 24; Adobe, Tukinoto, cover, 1; Shutterstock, FOOSKOOS, cover, 1, 22; Adobe, tabon, 3, 9, 11, 14, 18; Shutterstock, Natalia Rapoport, 5; Shutterstock, Ronnysteve, 6–7; Shutterstock, evaurban, 9; Shutterstock, isabel kendzior, 10–11; Shutterstock, Edwin Butter, 13, 21, 22; Shutterstock, evaurban, 14; Shutterstock, Elena Birkina, 18, 22; Shutterstock, Scalia Media, 20, 22; Shutterstock, Lizavetta, 21; Shutterstock, grayjay, 22; Shutterstock, BlueRingMedia, 22; Shutterstock, Diego Grandi, 22

Table of Contents

Meeting An Arctic Animal

Imagine walking outside in the winter. Snow crackles beneath your boots. Wind stings your face. Your coat keeps you warm.

You see a huge animal walking across the ice. It's white like the snow. A polar bear! It weighs as much as eight men and is longer than your bed. Polar bears live in the **Arctic**—one of the coldest places on Earth.

Polar Bear Watching

The polar bear has thick, warm fur. Its paws are as big as plates. You see its dark eyes and nose. The bear stands on its back legs. It's as tall as a basketball hoop.

POLAR POWER!

Polar bears have black skin to soak up heat from the sun.

POLAR POWER!

Polar bears have oily fur so water slides off and doesn't freeze.

You're cold! Polar bears have thick fat called **blubber** that keeps them warm. They have furry paws and claws to grip the ice. Their claws are as long as crayons.

The polar bear is quiet. Bears make sounds to **communicate**. Babies squeak and cry. Adults growl when they are angry.

POLAR POWER!

Polar bears also eat birds and eggs.

Looking for Food

The polar bear waits by a hole in the ice. A **seal** pops up for air. The bear grabs the seal and swallows it in big chunks.

Where Do Polar Bears Live?

Polar bears are excellent swimmers. They can swim for days. They rest on floating ice.

You see one bear. Polar bears often live alone. A group of bears is called a **sleuth**. Bears touch noses to ask for food. They play and fight.

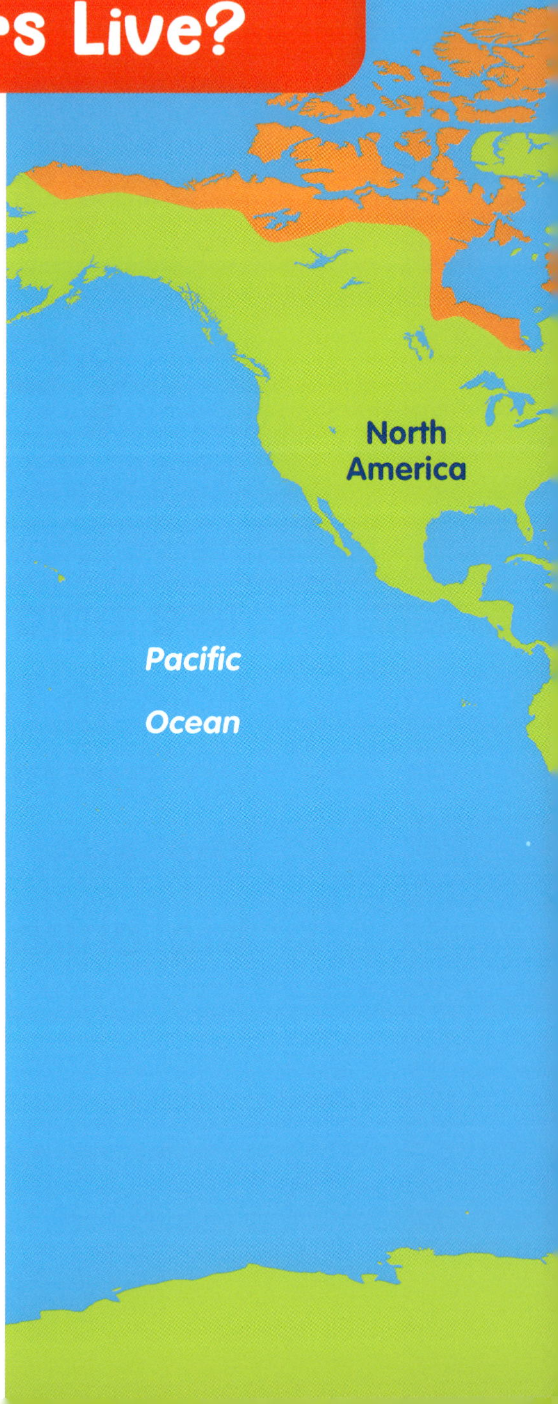

Arctic Ocean
Europe
Asia
Atlantic
Ocean
Pacific
Ocean
Africa
outh
erica
Indian
Ocean
Australia
KEY
Polar Bear habitat
Southern
Ocean
Antarctica

POLAR POWER!

Polar bears usually give birth to twins.

Polar Bear Families and the Future

You see babies! They were in their **den** in the snow. Baby bears are called **cubs**. Cubs are the size of a kitten when they are born.

Polar bears can live for 30 years. They need the snow and ice on Earth to survive. Someday you might see a real polar bear.

Parts of a Polar Bear

Teeth

Polar bears have 42 teeth. People only have 32. Polar bears have powerful bites and strong teeth. Their front teeth can grow as long as two paperclips.

Fur

Polar bear fur looks white but it is clear. Each hair is a tiny tube. The hairs trap warm air inside them. The trapped air works like a blanket to keep the bear warm.

Ears

Polar bears have small ears and good hearing. Their ears are furry outside and inside to protect against the cold.

Nose

Polar bears have an amazing sense of smell. They can sniff out a seal on the ice from 20 miles away.

Feet

Polar bears have big, flat, paws covered in fur. The fur keeps their feet warm and helps them walk on the slippery ice.

Glossary

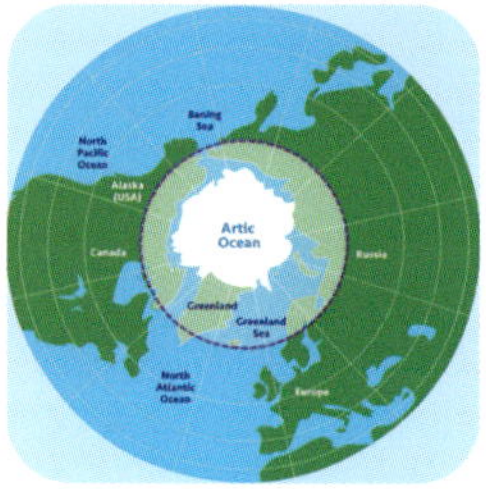

arctic (ARK-tik) a very cold place near the top of the Earth where there is lots of ice and snow

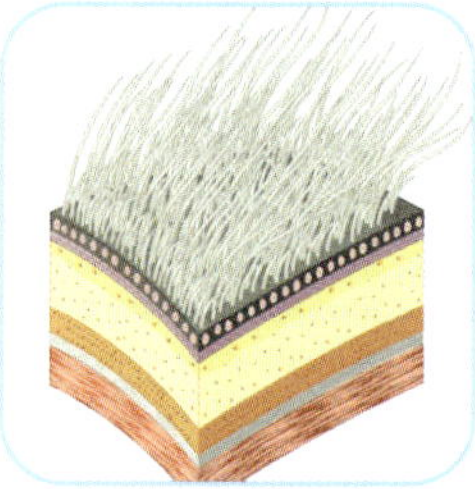

blubber (bluhb-er) a layer of fat under an animal's skin that keeps it warm

communicate (kuh-myoon-i-kayt) to share ideas or feelings by making sounds or movements

cub (kub) a baby polar bear

den (den) a safe place where an animal lives or rests

seal (seel) an animal that has flippers and swims in the ocean

sleuth (slooth) a group of polar bears

Quiz

1. **Do Polar Bears live in trees?**

   A. Yes B. No

2. **Do Polar Bears have warm fur?**

   A. Yes B. No

3. **Do Polar Bears eat penguins?**

   A. Yes B. No

4. **Are Polar Bear babies called cubs?**

   A. Yes B. No

ANSWER KEY:

1. No
2. Yes
3. No
4. Yes

Further Reading

Bowman, Chris. *Polar Bears.*
New York, NY: Scholastic, 2025.

Gibbons, Gail. *Polar Bears.*
New York, NY: Holiday House, 2025.

Kellett, Jenny. *The Ultimate Polar Bear Book.*
Melbourne, Australia: Bellanova Books, 2023.

On the Internet

Polar Bears

https://www.alaskazoo.org/polar-bear-camera
Watch the polar bears living at the Alaska Zoo.

Polar Bears

https://www.natgeokids.com/au/discover/animals/general-animals/polar-bear-facts/
Read more and see pictures of polar bears.

Polar Bear Sounds

https://polarbearsinternational.org/news-media/articles/decoding-polar-bear-vocalizations-den-behavior
Listen to the sounds polar bears make.

Index

About the Author

Kerrily Sapet has written more than 40 books for kids. She lives near Chicago with her family. Polar bears are one of her favorite animals. She wrote this book to learn more about them. Sapet has never seen any polar bears in the wild. She hopes to see one someday.